S0-DVV-516

The Word Is Love

By Sister M. Maura

INITIATE THE HEART

THE WORD IS LOVE

The Word Is Love

by SISTER M. MAURA, S.S.N.D.

The Macmillan Company · New York · 1958

First Printing

Library of Congress catalog card number: 58–11917

The Macmillan Company, New York
Brett-Macmillan Ltd., Galt, Ontario

Printed in the United States of America

From SPIRIT, A MAGAZINE OF POETRY published by the Catholic Poetry Society of America: "The Secret," "Bird in the Hand," © 1952; "Full Page Advertisement," © 1953; "Operation Return," "Navy Drill Yard," © 1954; "Dove with Olive Branch," "Data for Accreditation," "No Dirge for Dylan Thomas," "The Word I Learned," "Testament," "Rosary Processional," © 1955; "Polyphony Conventual" © 1956, all © by The Catholic Poetry Society of America, Inc.

Grateful acknowledgement is hereby made to ACCENT for permission to publish "Tourist in Dante"; to AMERICA for "We Walk in Miracles"; to the CATHOLIC ALUMNAE QUARTERLY for "Suggestion for a Gate of Heaven"; to THE CATHOLIC WORLD for "John at Patmos"; to THE MAGNIFICAT for permission to publish "Before First Holy Communion"; to NORTHERN REVIEW for "Desire Is a Falcon"; to POETRY CHAP BOOK for "Footnote for a Book of Mystics"; to THOUGHT for "Piece for a Museum"; to TODAY for "For a Class in Shakespeare"; to THE VIRGINIA QUARTERLY REVIEW for "Heritage"; and to VOICES for "Interlinear: Elegy for a Young Man."

Nihil Obstat: Rev. Edward A. Cerny, S.S., D.D.
Censor Librorum

April 18, 1958

Imprimatur: ✠ Francis P. Keough, D.D.
Archbishop of Baltimore

April 18, 1958

TO OUR LADY

CONTENTS

The Secret

The Child

The Cloister

The Secret

THE SECRET

In itself, this, of course, was not the secret:
Peter leaning sidewise incredulous to John,
and John against the shoulder hearing: he who takes
the bread that I have dipped. But the crumbs
of roasted flesh and the wild and bitter taste
of lettuce, this had bearing on the secret.

Not a tear upon the tendril of the rustling lintel leaves
but was bruised to sudden falling with the sound
of broken bread and the soundless prodigality
of words above the wine.
Not the mutter to the mutter, nor mouth to mouth,
nor mob to mob repeating that we have no king
but Caesar, this was not the secret.

But Androcles patient pulling at the thornspike
gestured toward it, and the little native
propping up the tailboard of the truck, picking at his nose
and looking at the linen, and the cleaner
circle riding on the fingers boned above the gold.

For the secret, nave and vaulting lift cathedrals
interlocking ages with the tenancy of faith:
secret laid upon the tempted tongue, timeless tongue;
secret offered on a junk and in a van; sewn in pockets;
suffered, savored, sanctuaried in the white of circumstance.

The point of all the arguments is round, of course.
It is the distance and the angle that create illusion
point as point (Dante peering up the wallribs
where the fixed stars all convene; or the anchoress
through the squint into the candled sanctuary;
or the Russian diplomat into the atomism of the microphone).

The point of all the arguments is round,
reflecting all the color of the spectrum, white
(not a fiber broken, not a tissue flayed),
and in our dullard patois—bread.

BIRD IN THE HAND

It must have been late dawn when the thrush curved his head
into the April air and incremental sunlight;
neophyte sheaths of song in the white breast,
the red-brown feather and wing bars spread;
touch of tree tops on the tail mumming the wind.

He was still warm in the hand
after the broken flight
into the deluding freedom of the closed east window.
He drowned in air at the impact,
like a plummeting graph.
Only the stain of feather on feather,
the sharp calligraphy of stiffening claws
for epitaph.

Bird in the hand? Rather two in bush,
three on branch, on bole; a flock in the glades;
the ponderous bequest of proverbs resigned to errata.

Whether restless wren hiving the privet hedge
or poor-grey mocking bird singing in the careful arcades
of thorn upon the lime,

or the foliation of the crimson head and breast
upon the half-decaying oak, the hammered sound
staccato on the headwind of the morning;

or the *kip, kip, kip,* from a cardinal mask,
or the iridescent grackle plucking worms from rain-pocked ground;

or the robin on the cherry tree—the cherry tree
like a toy, a varnished red and green
for posters for the Father of our Country—
the cherry tree where buttercups stand shouldering
the sunlight till the robins come and scatter sheen
of light to plunge of falling fruit
and scattered flight of robins in a dialect of spring;

even the crows—beaks still wet from plunder-fight;
or the brown and yellow back of the flicker,
or the sparrows never sold from creaturehood,
or the long *bob . . . white, bob . . . white*
from glittering grass in the swampy wood.

Here is a stunted heaven—bird in the hand.
One or many on bush or bole or bough,
rather than—feather on feather neatly folded
over the growing cold—bird in the hand now.

DESIRE IS A FALCON

Cathedral of Chartres. Right hand bay of north portal, "Squire with a falcon representing May. . . ."

Unhooded, the falcon clings
to the squire's hand,
stone plumage at rest,
taking command
from the boy who feeds
and restrains.

Two thousand years before the Christ,
legend tells
of falcon leashed to glove
by jess and bells.

What sculptor, garmented in grace,
conceived perennial of May
as "squire with a falcon"?
cutting in stone
the pull of flesh against the goad,
and curving bone
to grip the fingers while the beak,
lusting for plunder,
soberly feeds at the hand?

Come, heart, unthunder
August, and baffle the frost of January;
teach fingers to lock,

hold the peregrine falcon snugly
from shock
of old allures and older loves
of quarry meat.
Feed her heart,
on Wine, on Wheat.

FULL PAGE ADVERTISEMENT

Once it was ". . . a garden is
a lovesome thing . . . God wot . . ."
now a body is the lovely thing
(by implication—not

because it shelters, but because it is).
Satin page, in color too,
suggests directives to allure
by lift of eye or breast, by hue

of hair; by line of chin or leg
(and moderately priced in all details),
while vice sprawls on the curb of page
cheerfully paring his nails.

OPERATION RETURN

Now we have traded him back:
leaner, darker, sager,
the boy from Hopkins (varsity, lacrosse
and humanities major).

Jaw splayed to gritted teeth
against the fumbling stance,
he will be feted with therapy
and the sideways glance.

Because to dig he is not able,
and is yet unarmed to beg,
the best wood we give him:
poplar foot, and willow leg.

The continuous sweat of unlearning
will fortunately not be seen;
for litter cases and town welcome
consult the picture magazine.

TOURIST IN DANTE

Hell

He took the strata dome for comfort and
floodlights at night: Hell gate he saw and fire
outdid the myth of Hades, and he punned
the script—leave hope behind—for any bar.
The picture cards he bought he chose to gull
the rocker on the porch at home: the jaws
of Ugolino at the bishop's skull;
the Malebolge in flat color views;
another of the tidy giants' wall;
a mimic Hogarth of the hairy legs
of Lucifer; an abstract of the roll
and pitch of slothful clogged in mud like frogs.
And for himself a studio print he chose:
Democritus and Zeno called the wise.

Purgatory

He wearied of the terraces almost
immediately; disliked the hymnal rite,
the spiral tremor in the mountain crust
(no seismographic indication that
it could occur). The outworn shibboleth
of seven-three, the graven mountain side
he read, even the sculptured stone beneath
his feet, with clinical exactitude.
The too-bright traveling day revealed the catch,
the crowds, the tavern-like democracy.
A momentary thought of Malevich,
or Klee perhaps, soothed him as he saw
processional of candles, but light showed
the gryphon glorious. He caught the fraud.

Heaven

He dreaded most the gasp, the broken rune
of breath on breath. He clipped the traveler's mask
to mouth and nose but knew the oxygen
might fail. There was no one to ask. Star-discs
betrayed his sight. He thought he glimpsed a group
but it was all mercurial sound and light
honeycombing airy touchless slopes.
Somehow he was beyond the hurtling jet
of supersonic speed; he fought the rant
of choric peace, the native eloquent
propulsion toward an eye-unclouded point.
He could not wait to hail a taxi, flint
his lighter, suck a cigarette, get out
and to his room and drink a whiskey straight.

PROFESSOR OF MEDIEVAL BALLADRY

Forty years he has pursued his love.
By dilettantes at once amazed, perplexed,
he peers beyond them, over, back again,
probing the footnote text.

Upon the minstrel his scholarship broods;
sluicing an intricacy of word, he stares
abstractedly around the graduate seminar
till everyone nods back, and smiles, and shares.

He reads the ballads like an unselfconscious lover.
Suddenly with a "hey, nonny, nonny," his feet,
huge and forgotten underneath the desk,
pick up the ballad beat.

Once long, long ago, fishing in the creek
between his toes he oozed the sun-streaked mud;
no less warmly now there curls between his toes
Robin's greenwood, Edward's blood.

HERITAGE

> *It appears that the poems of Edward Taylor are unlike anything yet encountered in colonial American verse.*
>
> THOMAS JOHNSON

Southwest of Boston as the spear-ducks go
(ten decades of miles over river and land)
is his grave: *Edward Taylor, Learned &*
Pious Pastor. . . .
(When Donne died, the glow
audacious burned in Vaughan and Crashaw
still. It embered to ash
in fifty years.)
But the boy who came by slow
ship to Boston, spent the first great hours
with Increase Mather, then to Harvard with
young Samuel Sewall—at what local smith
had he blown the bellows? caught the showers
of spark in his commonplace book?
saw the dove on the casement ledge and dared to look?

And he *Served God and His Generation*
Faithfully for Many Years. But never told
them of the book. Gave his body in an affirmation
of belief—in fire, smallpox, massacre—
gave them salves and courage, simples and old
herbs. But never told them of the book.

He had the book. And God had him.
Once at thy Feast I saw thee Pearle-like stand . . .
he knew the threefold scarlet wing of seraphim,
and ate the dryness of desire in the land
of Massachusetts. *My bowl is but an acorn cup.*

His dialectic tempter—mind alone—
darker by far than any coal pit stone
humbled his ecstasy, the final cry of soul,
my fireless flame. Lord, Lord, blow the coal.

The tombstone of the *Learned & Pious Pastor*
sinks a little when the river rises. And
at Yale young men pursue the text (400 pages cast
in Puritan script). It was his grandson,
Ezra Stiles, gave it to the college.

Better he left gear and goods for children to share—
matchlock, bed, psalmbook, vat of tallow soap—
and mystery kept for the latter-day heir:
a man's book—rapture, anguish, seeking, seeing—
obscure to himself, secret and ciphered hope,
mere heritage of being.

NAVY DRILL YARD: UNIVERSITY CAMPUS

How many years after the frangible victory?
We have all forgotten. The men
with wired arms and poplar legs remember.

The hollow iron mast rises nearly upright
from concrete that covers the hot
corn-growing, Indiana soil.
Here the ensigns cursed the heat and sun,
stared into the imaginary mizzen,
hauled clew lines against the pitch and stress
of orders barked unendingly.

No waves scuttle against the cement
of the drill yard; no heaving gives the mast
a rake to stern; no combatants, cruisers
or patrols suck at the rudderstock.

Now only students stare out the window
of the Fine Arts Building—eyes running a ratline
to the crosstree, to the crow's-nest.
Ahab claws the morning light for sign
of the white whale, and Henry's little cabin boy
stands reeling in his sleep
and on a more luminous day
Raphael, angel of Tobias, smiles
over this present land—the healing gall
and liver of the fish within his hand.

The Child

BEFORE FIRST HOLY COMMUNION

The child looked up with wide, incurious eyes,
letting wonder trace
a way upon the nun's black veil, white coif,
serenities of a familiar face.

And the nun looked down, holding the arch
of veil above the child.
Her hands lifted the moist spirals of hair
from the warm wild
softness of curls. Ribbons and hair twisted;
the nun's hands were numb
before the face to Light uplifted,
the eyes' so eager *come*.

The child looked down to verify the prayer
of finger tips to finger tips,
and the nun saw hunger for God, like breath,
upon unvisited but parted lips.

DOVE WITH OLIVE BRANCH

I know that she is fearful
going home alone at night,
comely-young and dark-skinned
as Solomon's Sulamite.

I know that she has seen
more than has been said,
of rapine and purchase
and the house light's red.

Out of the text I discourse,
". . . integrity of soul . . ."
look down upon her innocence,
and am made whole.

Book upon book we plunder
for truth—white hand and dark—
in the city-of-God-on-campus,
the distaff-constant ark.

We who know the sound
of dyke and dune flood-broken,
remember the dove that Noah freed
to ask for God's peace-token.

And soon we shall send her out
in storm-ominous weather,
our plea and her promise united:
dove and olive branch together.

DATA FOR ACCREDITATION

Eighty-five acre campus . . .
outdoor swimming pool . . .
liberal arts plus vocational skills . . .
a better-than-average school.

Nodding, they swirl by the cloisters,
obviously hiding the suntan cream. . . .
How make the stuff of martyrs
out of this lunch hour stream?

How teach that the flask is venomed
and flaking with rust?
the body chambered for children?
and pride more vicious than lust?

Modestly, past the cloisters
the guileless sunbathers stream;
how shall we suffer beatitude
truncate this noonday dream?

Eighty-five acre campus. . . .
Out of our penance and pain,
accredit us, God, with mercy.
Grow, Thou, the grain.

INTERLINEAR: ELEGY FOR A YOUNG MAN

The Mother remembered how he had cut out paper snowflakes,
the paper creased and crossed in angles less acute
than blurred. But it didn't really matter for his blunted scissors
followed pleats and cornices in polarized pursuit.

Snow crystals smelled the air,
though none had fallen yet.
He decided to put the chains on the tires
before the roads were wet.

How his childhood fingers had opened the paper crystals
on the kitchen table; how he laughed and tossed
about the locked hexagonal stars; how the winter sun
was lavish on his thick unmelting heraldry of frost.

Between bride and groom the windshield glass
and epithalamion-refrains.
He pulled his happy vision down
to lock the tires with the chains.

No ice on branches of air so perfectly assumed
as this wobbly consonance of honeycomb design;
this stenciling of snowflakes in the tame emerald sunlight,
and the boy absorbed in acquiescent miracles of line.

The truck careened around the corner.
They never showed his body to his bride:

chaotic flesh and wardrobe montage,
and, unattached, the hand neatly flung aside.

Between the child cutting crystallines from drawing paper
and the young man home from his Pacific stint
and smiling at his bride, the smell of snow was on the air,
the frost unseasonal which grey skies hint.

Now snow like an unexpected mirror-image
is cryptic petrifaction of a grief
less real than the remembered boy in sunlight
cutting snowflakes in a wonder of belief.

CLASS IN SURVEYING

They are dispersed along the campus
like awkward, lately-planted trees;
breathing hoar against November afternoons,
they brace their measuring poles against their knees.

It is an old, an honorable calling.
In Egypt and in Greece it was at man's command.
Small boys read in tentative American histories,
George Washington surveyed Ohio land.

It is less easy, not less honorable for them now.
The tall boy crouched to the theodolite
calls, "O.K.," and folds the tripod;
the boys with poles carry the bright

landscape casually in their calculation notebooks.
Having been to Okinawa, Munich, Greenland and Rome,
they graph upon this pastoral campus grave young plans,
durable with vision and the promise of home.

PIECE FOR A MUSEUM

From the better home (and the better garden)
and the better college
the girls come. Baptized in subjunctive mood
of knowledge
confirmed (in the genteel church of art)
with current *mot juste,*
and dressed in Sunday advertisements:
nylon and cashmere musts.

Gallery silence is discreet, if not holy,
monk's cloth walls dignified;
the psalter is crisp and deckle-edged:
MUSEUM GUIDE.
Here, the daughter of the "lonely crowd"
takes communion with a new abstract;
eyes half closed, makes genuflection
to an artifact.

SING MAGNIFICAT

When the mock roses are in bloom
and our father, Saint Augustine, comes
like some noble pilgrim in the August liturgy,
petunias are primly flamboyant; bee hums
trundle lyrics into the noonday;
sky is shell-patterned in frugalities of white,
spruce and yew are snuffed in heat;
late summer in parentheses of sunny light.

Then she walks into our cloister—this young girl—
her laughter caught midsong;
freckles on her nose and cheekbones,
small hands brown, quick and strong.
A little awkward with the long black dress,
shaken and eager over each detail:
the heavy shoes and this new warmth of stocking,
the gentle ultimatum of the veil.

Father in heaven, by every sanction of our love,
we send petitions like new palmers to the altar gate:
O teach her heart the wisdom of the Pater Noster;
her feet the patience that will wait;
her eyes to countersign their facile seeking;
her hands to love the cloister of her sleeves' small dark;
O teach her heart the cadence of this old Magnificat we sing
to welcome her within this new and Dove-signed ark.

FOR A CLASS IN SHAKESPEARE

Bordered between
grill work of sun and shade,
and the powdery black board
with chalk dust trayed;
the worn words of prayer
we use as grace;
the weighted-with-wonder
commonplace
of opening text
bookmarked with letter and note
pulse the morning,
a psalm in my throat.

Hamlet's inconclusive pain,
Falstaff's roar,
Desdemona's tears are on our lips,
dozens of times we have read it before,
it is always new.

The bell will ring,
take grief and joy
and bantering
from out our speech.
But the words are there
under your cap
of child-bright hair.

Never again shall we need to say:
". . . and so—the play ends."
Forever, the book lies open
between us, friends.

NO DIRGE FOR DYLAN THOMAS

There are four great elegies, I tell my students,
(and this no gloss on any one of them)
bell branch lamentations for the singer,
encumbered stars blown from a pastoral stem.

God is patient with His poets,
Eden-lonely, bruised to anger and surprise,
aware of each historic leaf, and tavern-joy,
the festering bat, the clamorous eyes.

God's sun is blooming loudest now for Dylan Thomas,
rage, rage, is coppery colored in a spire;
the tumbledown tongue is prodigal home;
light breaks from secret, dark desire.

There are four great elegies—it does not really matter.
And this no dirge for singer, nor songs he never wrote.
Lament for song (I tell you this, my students)
that I should ever cause to dry within your throat.

The Cloister

AFTERNOON AT THE SHORE

Dragon and deep, praise the Lord . . .
PSALM 148

Her cloister walk, her academic discipline
are kilted up within her habit hem.
Beyond the sea wall, on the ramp of sand
the dog had wheedled them
for the afternoon. Now he begs for sticks
to be thrown in the water, and he swims
with a reckless sequence of ripples and sound,
and retrieves. The paw print limns
his awkward and untiring love
upon the sand. He shakes the river from the wet
dark feathers of fur; his coat blows dry
and dark red-gold, leaving a sandy fret
on the nun's ballooning habit and her veil.
Some winter twilight, in rubric of the Office,
she will kneel and rise
chanting: "Dragon and deep, praise the Lord . . ."
quiet laughter in her eyes.

FLIGHT IN AUTUMN

"Look, oh look," I heard you call,
"the geese are going south."
We leaned upon the garden wall;
behind your tilted head
your upturned hand, I stared
into the thin shellac of sun
upon the oaks. I dared
not say I could not find the darkened wedge
against the skies.
You turned grey, guileless eyes
to me and then I saw
the flight of geese,
the pattern of the primal law.

"And did you hear," you said,
"the strange wild sound they made?"
I who stirred
one moment too late
for cry or wing
of any live thing,
I had not heard.

But I could share
the startled breath upon your words,
the gentle touch of buoyant hand
curved to ancient rite of birds;

know the sound of open feather,
the headlong cry on brittle weather:
feel autumn on my eyes and mouth;
hear and see the geese fly south.

SUGGESTION FOR A GATE OF HEAVEN

When the nuns—a peach-bloom day of summer—
are invited to a picnic at someone's nearby shore,
they wear old, docile habits, faded veils,
and shoes grown comfortable and shabby long before.

Between the river and the thin, ungainly trees,
there is a mild lawn of beach-green grass
where pegs and hoops are set. One by one
with careful casualness the sisters pass

and then come back, kilting their skirts
and taking a tentative, counterfeit swing
with the mallet. Some of them remember
other years and other lawns: the sting

of starch in white shirt waists, the feel
of smoothness in the skirt, the heady pompadour.
Being awkward now, they laugh and are at ease.
"Your turn . . . one point . . . who's keeping score? . . ."

The sun is pliable and warm on ball and mallet,
the wind takes contour of the little group;
and they—"unless ye be as children"—
enter heaven through a croquet hoop.

FOOTNOTE FOR A BOOK OF MYSTICS

Mystic: a word too loosely flung about,
Whitman and Hopkins, Melville and Donne
and every other man who sometime dared
to look upon the sun.

"The Flaming Heart," "The Tiger," and "The Temple,"
something each poet must have known,
struck some angle of aperture and clung there
staring at the throne.

One more thing—let this relevant detail
be added to the mystics' book:
the lay sister doling food to dissipated men
and finding Christ in every look.

THE PASSION OF CHRIST

She who was wimpled and coifed
decorously yesterday,
walked in the cloister this evening,
in terrible disarray:

hands in gesticulation;
veil awry;
terror leaping like a flushed, young bird
from eye to eye;

lips poised to silence,
open and broken;
Ophelia songs dissonant;
nothing unspoken.

Once she had taken the cross;
now she was given the crown
of thorns; her habit a witness to
His purple gown.

One, bereft of reason,
who shall decry?
In the Body of Christ, in this Passion
are you and I.

CHRISTMAS: CONVENT INFIRMARY

Days before Christmas the cedars are set up.
It takes longer here to prepare—
for the fumbling steps and shaking hands need rest
and gentleness and care.

The best of the carefully mended conventual clothing,
trembling hands arrange and rearrange
on the bed for wearing to Christmas Mass.
And everything is strange

and new to the filmed eyes that see the past
more clearly than today.
The pulse is unsteady, but old, old prayers
move their accustomed way

unerringly as death. Ah, but the Child will come
carried by paten and candle and bell,
and tired bodies will echo *gloria, gloria*
fragile and constant as an ocean shell.

JOHN AT PATMOS

Half a yard of the bolt of winter sun
comes in the window lighting the aluminum stand
with its delicate, empty basket. Later
the glucose jar will snugly fit the sterile rind.

In the white conventual bed the old nun
has been waiting for seven days. Skin and flesh
recede to the desperate line of bone.
The blistered tongue quivers to the frailest lash

of breath. Only one hand is left to twitch at veil
and sheet; one hand to grip the crucifix;
one hand to grope at air. And no voice
at all. Only the eyes speak.

Above the bed is a bright print—*John at Patmos.*
John who saw the Lamb. Again and fearful again
the nun's eyes climb the grey wall
to the picture, only falling slowly down

to the grieving faces of her sisters to confide
the terrible consolation of God.

THE WORD I LEARNED

The word I learned to rhyme with *breath*
was *now-and-at-the-hour-of-our-death.*
Death, the word, did not seem odd
taught by a Sister—wed to God—
the word I could not understand,
like *apple, Christmas, book* and *hand.*
When grandpa was not in his chair
with lullabies and jumbled prayer,
and I was free from school to go
and watch his coffin down through snow,
breath I could touch in rise and fall,
the other word they said was a *call.*
Then *breath* was the distance from sleep to waking,
the other the hurt in my pulse-beat quaking:
the distance spanned, what I had seen
from the "Visitors" door to the hospital screen.
The word I used to rhyme with *breath*
is love of my Father, is unshaken feather
held to the lips; unspoken word on parted lips;
is blessed wax clinging to cold finger tips.
What it means I do not know,
but hour by hour I quietly go
to the word where Mother is, and grandpa, and friend,
where song has neither beginning nor end.
For need of a rhyme with the lovely word *breath*
nothing is better than loosing the tether

and running like hope or like thought
from the things they are teaching to the exquisite TAUGHT,
saying over and over with every breath
now-and-at-the-hour-of-our-death.

TESTAMENT

Never think she taught you knowledge, wisdom:
glossing the text of *Lycidas* with beauty,
nor *Canterbury Tales* with April pipes of joy,
saying, ". . . life, too, is a pilgrimage of . . ."

If ever she has taught you, it is now,
when looking gravely down,
(you, accustomed to looking up to lectern)
upon her mouth already livid with the promise of decay,
fingers clawed upon the vows,
the wimple much too stiff for classroom teaching,
you turn your eyes away.

Here she speaks her valediction,
to you so lyric girls in academic dress,
and you, young-bosomed matrons
with the smallest holding tightly to your fingers,
and you, mothers of the matrons, who learned
the dialect of love from her fruitful barrenness.

Under the thick, high-shouldered trees,
you take your orals on her teaching,
while locusts defeat
the summer silences, and wrens and mockingbirds
delirious with feathery sunlight
alliterate September heat.

Chanting the *Benedicite* responses,
you, her students, know the wise
are fools (in shallow coffins waiting the quick mold rotting)
while her tall soul walks seven terraces,
singing toward Paradise.

ROSARY PROCESSIONAL

This is not a background picturesque:
(flats and sets) for cloister garth in novel or in play:
suggestion of the medieval in the costume; frustration in the spirit;
"sad and serene" in a half-resisted, half-desired hideaway.

Curl of a copper-foil moon
on a hemlock tree; no stars. The starched white frame
of wimple and of veil a cyclotron
where ash-grey, jewel wings cavort in candle flame
warm, stammering light.

The nuns walk in processional
between the hydrangea blossoms cowled in heat,
crisp holly and smooth-leaved rhododendron shrubs.
Twigs and broken brush snap like puppies at the slow-paced feet;
wax melts to candle wivern and to gargoyle.

The nuns pray, "Hail Mary . . . Holy Mary . . ."
and the valley prays; the tennis courts, the parking lot;
terrace and lawn and road; the sweet gum prays;
the hawthorn; Spanish oak, yew and maple tree; the knot
of new-born mockingbirds nesting in the lime; a family of owls,
the squirrels, the kitten and the dog. "Hail Mary, full of grace . . .
Holy Mary . . ."

This is nothing like the neat enclosure
(sets and flats) of Spanish "Cradle Song," or—French and quaint—

the nuns of "Cyrano de Bergerac." These are not nuns of time or place
but God.

Queen and lady, though nuns and night and prayer
are mummers at your throne, it is you who walk with them,
it is you who carry Light—a quiet semaphore to God;
it is your country lane they walk; your Bethlehem;
your Nazareth; Gethsemane, and Ephesus.

Lady, it is your silence
in which they walk back to the cloister, to stifling cell,
and hot and heavy muslin of the bed.

Lady, it is your joy
that rocks the campus like a cradle
through the summer night, so that the Little Boy
(still in exile) does not weep,
but laughs in His Father's providence, and falls
(as Péguy says men should) content to sleep.

SUGGESTION FOR A NUN'S OBITUARY

Be brief with eulogistic speech,
recording blueprints of her labor;
cautious of the gospel of her calvaries,
the foothills of her Thabor.

In her no radiance could be seen:
ember and ash, but rarely fire.
Write this: God loved her, and
greatly she desired to desire.

POLYPHONY CONVENTUAL

My weight is love.
St. Augustine

With voluminous renaissance sleeves rolled back,
the sister leans over the child making paper hills
and a paper moon—red and orange—on black
with flour-and-water paste clamoring everywhere.

Or with a riddle-me-this eyebrow raised to coif line,
studies petrifaction of the myth
to the permanence of marzipan
and the cocktail hour topography of little magazines.

Iconoclast of the magic mirror on the wall
and mannequins antiphonal in the small salon,
she admonishes the memory to seven mansions
and the crystal center—God. But (Alice said
in a thoughtful tone, "That's a great deal
to make one word mean") the bridal bed
is in the canticle.

She could, of course, kilt a too-thread-mended habit
to handling the ubiquity of dust,
the waspish regularities of convention, decorum and waxed floors.

And appear incongruous at fashionable lectures
and congruous to birthdays without landmarks.
She makes tranquil the activity of her anchorhold
like Roger Bacon's on a bridge above the Thames.

Alchemist, she has a private (not written)
Book of Beasts snared from psalm, exempla,
and churlish affinity of dear flesh.

Learning is lonely. And not with a delicate aloneness
like the Celtic monk with Panguar-White, contemplative cat,
who would, after all, not be pleased any more than she
with Faculty Tea.

Reason and audacity pillage the minutes of meditation;
how blow live coal, lips still raw with charred flesh.

Discipline tied carefully, like an apron,
on remembrance, keeps the day hours neat.
Night is an undiscovered country from whose bourne
this traveler returns a few times
that the compassionate saints may pull
the gravitation to the dictum of Augustine.

WE WALK IN MIRACLES

We walk in miracles as children scuff
through daisy fields, their dresses appliquéd
with shifting tide of blossom, welkin-stuff,
the Father's white creative laughter made.

Common as spring, as bread, as sleep, as salt,
the daisies grow. Our Father made them reel
against us like the morning stars that vault
the greater home His love will yet reveal.

The petals push against the ankles, knees,
the thigh, the hands; gold pollen sifts within
the pores to rivulets of veins, to seas
of subtle life behind unsubtle skin.

O deeper and deeper than daisy fields, we drown
in miracles, in God, our Seed, our Crown.